The Merriest Christmas Book

MARK LINK, S.J.

ARGUS COMMUNICATIONS
7440 NATCHEZ AVENUE · NILES, ILLINOIS 60648

CONTENTS

ACKNOWLEDGEMENTS

From *the death of Christmas* by Kenan Heise and Arthur R. Allan © copyright 1971 The Death of Christmas Book Fund. Reprinted by permission from Kenan Heise. *the death of Christmas* may be purchased for $1.50 from the Illinois Department of Public Aid, 624 S. Michigan Avenue, Chicago, Illinois 60605. All proceeds from the sale of this book to go to the Neediest Children's Christmas Fund.

From "Let's Give Christmas Back to the Pagans" by Peter Riga, *U.S. Catholic*, December, 1971. Reprinted by permission from *U.S. Catholic*.

From "The Wise and the Prodigal" by Robert G. Wells, *The Milwaukee Journal*, December 23, 1960. Reprinted by permission of *The Milwaukee Journal*.

From "When Christmas Was Banned in Boston" by Dana P. Marriott, *American Heritage* © 1967. American Heritage Publishing Company, Inc. Reprinted by permission from *American Heritage* (December, 1967).

From "Pretty Well Picked Over" by Mike Royko, *Chicago Daily News*. Reprinted by permission of Mike Royko.

From Gene Symonds, United Press International, December 24, 1950. Reprinted by permission of United Press International.

From "The Origins of the Christmas Liturgy" by Aelred Tegels, *The Bible Today*, December, 1962. Reprinted by permission of *The Bible Today*.

From "The Prayer of the Donkey" from *Prayers from the Ark* by Carmen Bernos de Gasztold, translated by Rumer Godden. English text: Copyright © 1962 by Rumer Godden. Reprinted by permission of The Viking Press, Inc.

From "Christmas In Other Lands" by Margaret Mead. Reprinted from *Redbook Magazine*, December, 1965, copyright © The Redbook Publishing Company.

From *The Homecoming: A Novel About Spencer's Mountain*, by Earl Hamner, Jr. Copyright © 1970 by Earl Hamner, Jr. Reprinted by permission of Random House, Inc.

From *A New Look at Christmas Decorations* by Sister Maria Gratia Listaite and Norbert Hildebrand Copyright © The Bruce Pbulishing Company 1957. Reprinted by permission of Macmillan Publishing Company.

From "Panic in a Pear Tree," *Life Magazine*, December 15, 1972. *Life Magazine*, © 1972 TIme Inc. Reprinted with permission.

From *Christmas in Germany* by William H. Crawford, Jr. Copyright 1949 by Oxford University Press, Inc. Reprinted by permission.

From "Why Keep On Celebrating Christmas?" by Joseph Blenkinsopp, *Commonweal*, December 24, 1971. Reprinted by permission of *Commonweal*.

From *The Catholic Digest*, December, 1971. Reprinted by permission.

From "Where Santa Comes by Troika" by Tobi Frankel, *McCall's Magazine*, December, 1964. Reprinted by permission of *McCall's Magazine*.

From "Santa's Country," *Holiday Magazine*, December, 1971. Reprinted with permission from *Holiday Magazine* © 1971 The Curtis Publishing Company.

From *The Year of Our Lord in the Christian Home* by Francis X. Weiser. Published by The Liturgical Press Copyrighted by The Order of St. Benedict, Inc. Collegeville, Minnesota.

From "Christmas Letter from Australia" by Douglas B.W. Sladen from *The Australian Christmas* by F. Cusack. Reprinted by permission of Heinemann Publishing Company, Melbourne, Australia.

From *Holidays in Wales* by William H. Crawford, Jr. Copyright 1950 by Oxford University Press, Inc. Reprinted by permission.

From *The Book of Christmas* by Marguerite Ickis. Reprinted by permission of Dodd, Mead & Company.

From The Life Book of Christmas, Volume Three. *The Merriment of Christmas* courtesy Time-Life Books.

From *Chimney-Pot Papers* by Charles S. Brooks. Reprinted by permission of Yale University Press.

From "About This Issue," *Harper's Magazine*, Copyright 1971 by *Harper's Magazine*. Reprinted from the December, 1971 issue by special permission.

From "Epstein, Spare That Yule Log!" from *Verses from 1929 On* by Ogden Nash. Copyright 1933 by Ogden Nash. Reprinted by permission of Little, Brown and Co.

From *The Christmas Book*, copyright, 1952, by Francis X. Weiser. Reprinted by permission of Harcourt Brace Jovanovich, Inc.

From *The Life of Christ* by Giuseppe Ricciotti. Translated by Alba Zizzamia. © Copyright 1947, 1952 by The Bruce Publishing Company. Reprinted by permission of Macmillan Publishing Company.

From "The Years in Galilee" by Howard LaFay, *Everyday Life in Bible Times*. Reprinted by permission of The National Geographic Society.

Excerpt from p. 68 in *The Day Christ Died* by Jim Bishop Copyright 1957 by Jim Bishop. By permission of Harper & Row, Publishers, Inc.

From *St. Bernard's Sermons for the Seasons and Principal Feasts of the Year*, Volume I. Reprinted by permission of The Paulist Press.

From Associated Press Newsfeatures, December 25, 1973. Reprinted by permission.

From *The Graces of Christmas* by Bernard Wuellner, S.J. Copyright © Bernard Wuellner, S.J. 1958. Reprinted by permission of Macmillan Publishing Company.

From "Prayer for Direction" by Helen Louise Welshimer from *50 Years of Christmas* by R.M. Elmquist. Reprinted by permission of *The Christian Herald*.

From "The Shepherds at the Crib—A Lucan Vignette" by Roger Mercurio, *The Bible Today*, December, 1962. Reprinted by permission of *The Bible Today*.

From "Prayer of a Roman Soldier" by Nick Iuppa, *The Sign Magazine*, December, 1972. Reprinted by permission of *The Sign Magazine*, Union City, N.J.

From "Star of the Nativity" by Boris Pasternak from *The Poems of Doctor Zhivago*. Translated by Eugene M. Kayden. Reprinted by permission and courtesy of Eugene M. Kayden.

From "Christmas really is a humbug" by Andrew Greely, *The Chicago Tribune*, December 25, 1973. Reprinted by permission of Andrew Greely.

From "Let's Keep the Tinsel in Christmas" by Richard Frisbie, *U.S. Catholic*, December, 1972. Reprinted with permission from *U.S. Catholic*.

From "Sounding Board" by James A. Dunn, *U.S. Catholic*, December, 1971. Reprinted with permission from *U.S. Catholic*.

From "Sounding Board" by Martin Kenny, *U.S. Catholic*, December, 1972. Reprinted with permission from *U.S. Catholic*.

From "Hospital Christmas" by Catherine Lanham Miller, *Good Housekeeping Magazine*. Adapted from *How to Say Yes to Life: A Woman's Guide to Beating the Blahs* by Catherine Lanham Miller. Reprinted by permission from the December, 1971, issue of *Good Housekeeping Magazine*. © 1971 by The Hearst Corporation.

From "Sounding Board" by John Crosby, *U.S. Catholic*, December, 1972. Reprinted with permission of *U.S. Catholic*.

From "Peter, Me & Mary" by Bob Combs and Scott Ross, *Campus Life Magazine*, May, 1972. Originally published as "Paul and" in *Free Love*. Freeville, N.Y. 13068. Reprinted by permission of Bob Combs.

Reprinted with permission from *Prayer From Where You Are* by James Carroll. Copyright 1970. Published by Pflaum Publishing.

From *Instant Replay: The Green Bay Diary of Jerry Kramer* by Jerry Kramer. Reprinted by permission of The New American Library.

From *The Taste of New Wine* by Keith Miller. Reprinted by permission of Word, Inc., Waco, Texas.

From "What Shall We Give the Children?", *McCalls Magazine*, December, 1964. Reprinted by permission of *McCalls Magazine*.

Excerpt from p. 142 in *Strength to Love* by Martin Luther King, Jr. Copyright © 1963 by Martin Luther King, Jr. By permission of Harper & Row, Publishers, Inc.

From "A Garland of Wishes for the Seven Ages of Christmas" by Margaret Cousins, *McCalls Magazine*, December, 1968. Reprinted by permission of *McCalls Magazine*.

DESIGN BY GENE TARPEY

PHOTO CREDITS

Gene Ahrens 67B, 69, 98, 111
Mary Baber 21, 32, 96B
Mark Barinholtz/VAN CLEVE Photography 93
G. Matthew Brady/Tom Stack & Associates 31
Carol Ann Bales 64
Tod Brennan 16–17
John Dylong 63, 94–95, 120
William R. Eastman/Tom Stack & Associates 70, 97T
John W. Glaser 116, 117L, 117R
Sid Grapey 35, 36, 80
Algirdas Grigaitis Cover, 2, 9, 42T, 57
Adeline Haaga/Tom Stack & Associates 12B, 33B
Nancy Hamilton/VAN CLEVE Photography 54
Thomas A. Henley/Tom Stack & Associates 55R, 58
Robert Hollis 34
Brent M. Jones 45B

Earl Kubis/Tom Stack & Associates 65
Bill Noel Kleeman/Tom Stack & Associates 75
Jean-Claude LeJeune 8, 25, 30B, 33T, 52, 56, 66, 77, 100
Robert M. Lightfoot III/VAN CLEVE Photography 51
Mark Link 73, 79T, 84
Sister Mary Lucas 37, 72, 112
Steve Matalon 24B
Bob McKendrick 18L, 27, 59, 105, 119
Burton McNeely/VAN CLEVE Photography 40
Pat Murphy/Tom Stack & Associates 12T
Walt Oleksy/VAN CLEVE Photography 9
Jerome F. Riordan 74T, 81, 85B, 89T
Shirley Richards 74B, 90
David Rogers 45T
Joe Rychetnik/VAN CLEVE Photography 63

Paul Sequeira 20, 22, 43, 44T, 48T, 48B, 49, 82, 83, 101, 102B, 104, 107
C.B. Sharp/VAN CLEVE Photography 5
Dr. Phillip Sheridan/Tom Stack & Associates 68
Ken Short 28, 47, 87, 96T
Tom Stack/Tom Stack & Associates 110, 118
William H. Stribling/VAN CLEVE Photography 91
Olle Swartling 46
Gene Tarpey 6, 10, 11, 13, 14T, 14B, 15, 18T, 18R, 19, 24T, 26, 30T, 39, 41, 42B, 44B, 60, 61, 62, 76B, 78, 79B, 86, 89T, 89B, 92, 102T, 103, 108, 109, 113, 115
William Weaver 53
Richard Werle 29
Mark S. Wittenberg/Tom Stack & Associates 38

Argus Communications, 7440 Natchez Avenue, Niles, Illinois 60648

International Standard Book Number: 0-913592-33-1

INTRODUCTION

The merriest star
came out
when the sky
was the darkest.

Christmas Gifts

1
Today

A DILEMMA

WHAT'S HAPPENING, VIRGINIA?

"Last year I had seven dollars
to buy Christmas with."

The speaker, a mother of five,
epitomizes the Christmas dilemma
faced each year . . .
by millions of other Americans . . .

This dilemma consists of
trying to create
the appearance of Christmas for their children
without having the substance . . .

Kenan Heise and Arthur Allan
the death of Christmas

Does Christmas mean anything to people
any more?
or is it merely
"appearance without substance?"

I CAN'T EXPLAIN IT

parking lot attendant: Christmas is a joke. Maybe, it's okay for kids too dumb to know any better.

mother of seven: I didn't have anything as a kid. But I thought things might be different for my kids. Nothing has changed at all. If anything, it's gotten worse.

I know how bad it sounds, but I've come to hate Christmas. It's just another day when my kids find out they're different. TV just makes things worse. The kids get all those big ideas and hopes, only to have Christmas smash them.

You try to explain things to kids on Christmas. I can't do it anymore.

CHRISTMAS WALK

A midi coat is a must if you want your dog to be fashionably attired for a Christmas morning walk . . .
Rubber or plastic, boots protect paws from salt and chemicals on snowy streets.

Heise and Allan
the death of Christmas

9

LATE SPURTS

An extra shopping day
proved a Christmas bonus
for the nation's retailers last week . . .
Heaviest concentration
was in rtw [ready-to-wear]
and accessories,
with furs and jewelry
showing late spurts.

Heise and Allan
the death of Christmas

"IT'S ALL KINDA FUNNY . . ."

College girl: The churches aren't keeping Christmas
alive anymore. The stores and their
TV commercials are.

Let's face it. As a religious affair,
Christmas is dead. It's all kinda funny,
in a sick sort of way. Christmas was
supposed to celebrate Christ's birth,
not his death.

OVERHEARD

The sign read: PUT CHRIST INTO CHRISTMAS
                THIS YEAR.

A young lady glanced at it momentarily,
then, turned to her friend and said:

"Hmm! Now the Church is trying to poke her
nose into Christmas."

SUPERMARKET SIGN

Artificial Trees
  with
Authentic Christmas
  Spirit.

FOR SALE: CHRISTMAS

It seems but too evident to me
that modern commercial pagans have destroyed
not only the religious basis of this feast,
but also the human warmth and merriness
that grew up around it.
As Christians we should have the courage
to leave this lifeless carcass to the vultures of
commercialism and to choose another date
on which to celebrate the true meaning
of Christmas.

Peter Riga
"Let's Give Christmas Back to the Pagans"
U.S. Catholic

THE WISE
AND THE PRODIGAL

And it came to pass,
the season of the last minute shopper having come,
that it was Friday.
The time of desperation was upon the land and lo,
there was wailing and gnashing of teeth.

The wise shoppers departed homeward . . .
bearing with them gifts of exceeding worth,
to be paid for no man knew when.
The pleas to do such shopping
early had resounded loud in the land,
being cried from housetops
and trumpeted from the loudspeakers.

And it happened that the wise shoppers
had heeded these exhortations
so that in the time of desperation
their teeth should remain ungnashed and their garments unrent. . .

And so it was that the prodigal shopper appeared at the gates,
wild of eye and trembling, crying aloud to the merchants.

"Sell me anything," he was crying,
"sell me whatever is left. Sell me the gifts
the wise shoppers cast aside as unworthy, for there is no time
remaining. . ."

And it came to pass on the last Friday before the Sunday
that is called Christmas
that there were legions of such prodigals abroad in the land.
each trampling the other and striking out with his elbows.

And the wise men heard the noise and saw the confusion
and were exceedingly content.

Robert W. Wells
The Milwaukee Journal

SCROOGE

What's Christmas time to you
but
a time for paying bills without money;
a time for finding yourself a year older,
and not an hour richer . . .

If I had my will,
every idiot who goes around
with "Merry Christmas" on his lips
should be boiled in his own pudding
and buried
with a stake of holly through his heart.
He should!

Charles Dickens
A Christmas Carol

CHRISTMAS: banned in Boston

On May 11, 1659,
the legislature of the Massachusetts Bay Colony
enacted the following:

" . . . Whosoever shall be found observing any
such day as Christmas or the like,
either by forbearing of labour, feasting, or any other way,
upon any such account as aforesaid,
every such person so offending shall pay
for every such offence five shillings, as a fine to the
county."

. . .The cheerless law of 1659 remained on the books
for twenty-two years.

Dana P. Marriott
"When Christmas Was Banned in Boston"
American Heritage

TIS THE SEASON . . .

We are entering again
the annual season
of depression and neurosis:
the season of Christmas,
whose meaning has been perverted
so grossly
that it now causes manifest damage
to many human beings . . .

The Center for Studies
of Suicide Prevention has noted
that most of December's suicides
are centered around
the twenty-fifth of the month.

Peter Riga
"Let's Give Christmas Back to the Pagans"
U.S. Catholic

PRETTY WELL
PICKED OVER

The owner of a Michigan Avenue restaurant
called me with a problem
that frequently comes up at Christmas.

He had planned a party at his place for 100 needy
children. But for some reason he had
only half that many coming.

Now, with the party only two days off, he was
frantically trying to find an extra fifty
needy children.

"Do you know where I can get them?" he said.

I asked if he had tried an orphanage.
He hadn't, so I gave him the name of one.

He called back a few minutes later and said:
"No luck. They're already taken."

All I could do was suggest that he keep trying,
call orphanages and social agencies.

But I warned him to expect disappointment.
He had waited much too long. When you get down
to the last week before Christmas, the needy children—
especially orphans—
already have been pretty well picked over . . .

Last year, on Christmas Eve afternoon,
a very angry young woman called. She and some friends
had just rounded up old clothes and old toys
to give away, but couldn't find anyone to give them to.
They had called several social agencies but they
had closed for the day.

Knowing how upsetting such disappointment could be,
I tried to be helpful and suggested that they wait
until after Christmas when the social agencies
reopened, since the clothes and toys would be
needed, then, too.

"But Christmas will be over then," the woman said,
"and it won't be the same."

How true . . .

One should start thinking about these things
as early as Thanksgiving—or before,
if possible . . .

One of the problems in looking for someone
to good-deed is that there is no
convenient way to shop around . . .

What may be needed is some kind of special
Christmas catalog, such as Sears and Ward's
put out for their merchandise,
but containing instead a complete assortment of
the needy . . .

If people had something like that,
they could plan calmly and avoid the frantic,
last-minute rush to perform a good deed.

Best of all, there wouldn't be any disappointment.
Christmas comes but once a year,
and everyone should get a chance to do good.
It's such a long wait until next time.

Mike Royko
The Chicago Daily News

HOW PAUPERS SPEND CHRISTMAS

You come here to see how paupers
    the season of Christmas spend;
You come here to watch us feeding
    as they watch the captured beast

George Robert Sims
"Christmas Day in the Workhouse"

"IT SEEMS TO ME . . ."

suburban
high school boy:

My Mom says I'm going through a phase or something about Christmas. Maybe she's right. But, it seems to me, Christmas has become just a big advertising campaign.

I don't pretend to speak for all kids my age. You can only speak for yourself. But I bet a lot of them think like I do about Christmas.

TILL ANOTHER YEAR BE GONE!

High noon behind the tamarisks,
    the sun is hot above us—
As at home the Christmas Day is
    breaking wan,
They will drink our healths at dinner—
    those who tell us how they love us,
And forget us till another year be gone!

Rudyard Kipling
"Christmas in India"

"IT CHANGED
MY WHOLE VIEW"

19 year-old:

I've been on drugs, but now I'm making it.
I was really thinking of going home for Christmas,
but when I thought how my appearance and my views
have changed—how different I was—
I would have ruined their Christmas by showing up.
To them, it would have been like
inviting a bum off the street.
They would have thrown me out.
They cannot accept me for myself, the way I am now.

It was the Christmas that I was 15
when I learned the difference.
I had always gone along with a happy view of the occasion.
That year I bought a lot of gifts.
My Mom told me all the gifts I had bought were wrong.
I told her they were supposed to be gifts from
me to the family, not from her.
She slapped me and sent me to my room.
I had bought my little brother a toy and she told me
I should have bought him a jumpsuit.
It changed my whole view.

My fondest memory is still the smile
on my little brother's face when he got a gigantic candy cane.
The true meaning is everybody together and happy
and that's what I'd like to see.
In that sense, I'd think Christmas is the best idea in the world.

Heise and Allan
the death of Christmas

I WONDER . . .

Christmas eve here is a machine gun sitting on the
edge of your foxhole with the bolt back ready to go.
It's a pale, full moon casting grotesque shadows
among the fierce, rugged mountain peaks around you.
It's your buddy crouching in the bottom of a
freezing dugout
with a blanket around his shoulders to smoke a cigarette . . .

Out there, across those mountain peaks,
a few miles away, are the Communists.
They have been building up a long time
and tonight would be a nice time for them to strike . . .

The talk, what there is of it, is all of home:
"I wonder what the folks will be doing tonight?"
and "I wonder what Mary got the kids for Christmas?". . .

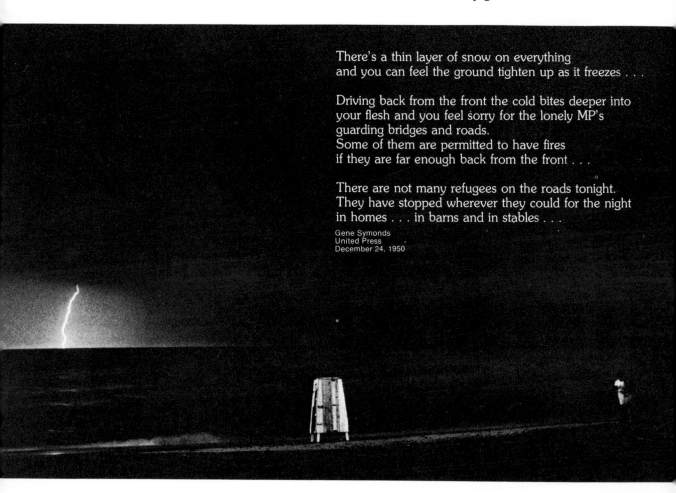

There's a thin layer of snow on everything
and you can feel the ground tighten up as it freezes . . .

Driving back from the front the cold bites deeper into
your flesh and you feel sorry for the lonely MP's
guarding bridges and roads.
Some of them are permitted to have fires
if they are far enough back from the front . . .

There are not many refugees on the roads tonight.
They have stopped wherever they could for the night
in homes . . . in barns and in stables . . .

Gene Symonds
United Press
December 24, 1950

IN A BAR
ON CHRISTMAS EVE

Jesus: I tell you a Christmas story you not believe.
You want to listen?

My mother lives in Puerto Rico.
Before I born, she make the "promisa."
That is like the oath. She promise to Virgin
if she get her wish granted, she name the next
baby after her or after her Son.
My mother get her wish. Then I born.
She call me Jesus Maria for good measure . . .

You still want to hear my story?
I tried drinking myself to death by becoming a
drunkard.
Never nobody loves me. I been lonely all my life . . .

I am now 55 years old and I am ready to wait
for death. I feel someone looks after me. . .
It is maybe because of the "promisa" and
because I have His name . . .

Heise and Allan
the death of Christmas

2
Yesterday

A TIME OF JOY

TINY TIM

Mrs. Crachit: And how did Tiny Tim behave?

Mr. Crachit: As good as gold. And better.
Somehow, he gets thoughtful,
sitting by himself so much,
and thinks the strangest thoughts
you ever heard.

He told me, coming home,
that he hoped the people saw him
in the church,
because he was a cripple,
and it might be pleasant to them
to remember, upon Christmas day,
who it was who made lame beggars
walk and blind men see.

Charles Dickens
A Christmas Carol

A MOMENT OF SEEING

We have all read what happened
between the opposing armies . . .
We hear of this sudden change
upon the night of Christmas Eve,
how there was singing upon one side
answered by the other . . .

Everyone who tells of it
speaks also of his own wonder,
as if he had seen a miracle . . .
as if the armies had been gathered together . . .
not for war but for the Christmas feast.

A. Clutton-Brock
The Times of London

A CHRISTMAS CARMEN

Blow, bugles of battle,
  the marches of peace;
East, west, north, south let
  the long quarrel cease;
Sing the song of great joy
  that angels began,
Sing the glory of God and
  of good-will to man!

John Greenleaf Whittier
"A Christmas Carmen"

CALL TO LIFE

To us this day is born a Savior.
Let us rejoice.
It would not be right to be sad today,
for today is Life's birthday,
the birthday of that Life which, for us,
takes away the sting of death
and brings the bright promise of an eternal
hereafter . . .

Rejoice if you are good,
for you are drawing nearer to your goal!
Rejoice if you are less than good,
for your Savior offers you pardon!
And if you are a non-believer rejoice,
for God calls you to life!

Pope St. Leo
"Christmas Homily"

BIRTHDAY OF THE SUN

The first reference . . .
to the feast of Christmas is found
in the so-called Roman Chronograph of 354,
an almanac copied and illustrated
by the famous Greek artist Philocalus . . .

This document
contains a rudimentary Christian calendar
in the form of two lists of dates . . .
At the head of the first list,
for December 25, we find . . .
"Birth of Christ in Bethlehem of Judea . . ."

The date of December 25
was deliberately chosen at Rome . . .
sometime between 274 and 336,
with the express purpose of countering
the influence of the pagan feast of
Sol Invictus, the Unconquerable Sun,
officially instituted in 274
by the Roman Emperor Aurelian . . .

From an anonymous treatise
dating from the third or early fourth century
[we read] . . .
"Now they call this day the
'Birthday of the Unconquerable!'
Who, indeed, is so unconquerable
as our Lord,
who overthrew and conquered death?
And as for talking about the birthday
of the Sun!
He is the Sun of Justice!
He whom the prophet Malachi said:

'For you who fear my name
there will arise the Sun of Justice,
with healing in its wings.'"

Aelred Tegels
"The Origins of the Christmas Liturgy"
The Bible Today

SO HALLOW'D THE TIME

Some say that ever 'gainst that season comes
Wherein our Saviour's birth is celebrated,
The bird of dawning singeth all night long:
And then, they say, no spirit can walk abroad;
The nights are wholesome; then no planets strike,
No fairy takes, nor witch has power to charm,
So hallow'd and so gracious is the time.

William Shakespeare
Hamlet, I, i

28

FRANCIS' CRIB

In a cave on a windswept Italian mountainside,
Francis of Assisi assembled the first
Christmas crib in 1223.
The Christ child, placed on an altar of stone,
and two live animals—an ox and a donkey—
were its only occupants.
Today, a tiny monastery surrounds the cave,
which still remains relatively undisturbed by the years.

The idea behind the crib was to make the
story of Christ's birth more vivid in the minds of
shepherds and farmers who lived there.
The people were enthusiastic.
They were the ones who suggested the ox and donkey.

Thomas of Celano, one of Francis' companions,
wrote about the opening of the crib:

"The friars from different localities had come.
The men and women of the place brought
candles and torches to illuminate the night.

Lastly the saint arrived, saw all the preparations,
and was happy.
The crib was put in place, the hay brought in,
and the ox and donkey were led forward.
Simplicity was honored, poverty exalted, humility
praised . . .

The woods rang with voices and the rocks echoed
the hymns of joy.
The saint, vested as the deacon of the Mass,
chanted the Gospel.
He preached to the people about the poor King of
Bethlehem.
At the end of the vigil, everyone returned to his
home full of joy."

PRAYER OF THE DONKEY

O God, who made me
to trudge along the road always,
to carry heavy loads always,
and to be beaten always;
Give me great courage and gentleness.
One day, let somebody understand me—
that I may no longer want to weep
because I can never say what I mean
and they make fun of me.
Let me find a juicy thistle—
and make them give me time to pick it.
And, Lord, let me find again, one day,
my little brother of the Christmas Crib.
Amen.

Carmen Bernos de Gasztold
"Prayer of the Donkey"

AMENDING THE PAST

In Mexican villages on the nine nights before Christmas,
people commemorate *Las Posadas*,
the journey of Mary and Joseph to Bethlehem and their vain search
for a resting place among all the travelers crowded into town . . .
Soon after dark the villagers gather and walk
in a long, winding procession through the streets,
carrying candles and accompanied by music
to bring the sacred figures to the home of the host for the night.
They knock at the door and ask for shelter, and now a peasant family
proudly makes reparation for the old refusal
by welcoming the Child.

Margaret Mead
"Christmas In Other Lands"
Redbook magazine

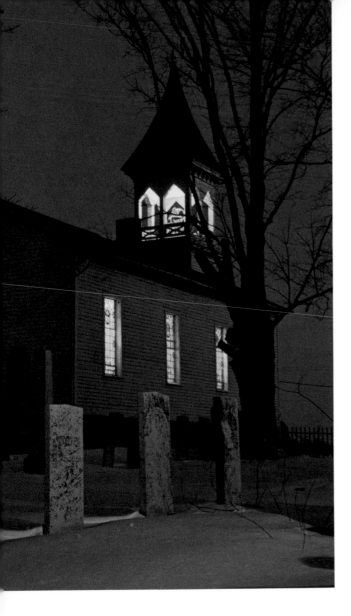

WHILE NIGHT
WAS IN THE MIDST
OF HER COURSE

When midnight, dark and still,
Wrapped in silence vale and hill:
God the Son, by Virgin's birth . . .
Began to live as man on earth.

Quando Noctis Medium
4th Century

Although the Gospel shrouds in secret
the hour of Jesus' birth,
Christian tradition sets the time as midnight.
The basis for this is rooted in
the Old Testament Book of Wisdom 18: 14–15:

"While all things were in quiet silence,
and the night
was in the midst of her course,
your almighty word
leapt down from heaven from your royal throne,
as a fierce conqueror
into the midst of the land of destruction."

Thus, midnight services on Christmas Eve
have been a tradition in many Christian churches
in the United States and Europe.
In Spain, Midnight Mass
climaxes with people parading in the streets
with torches and guitars.
In Germany, it becomes the occasion for
solemnly placing the Infant in the church crib.

CHRISTMAS CAROLS

Our English word "carol"
takes us journeying backwards
into the misty Middle Ages.
Referring to a circle dance, accompanied by song,
it would probably remind us
of children's "ring-around-a-rosy."
The origin of this kind of dance
goes back to Greek times.

Chaucer refers to it in one of his works:
"And I, withoute tarrying
Went into the caroling."

Today,
the word "carol" refers to singing only.

OLD ENGLISH CAROL

In a manger laid and wrapp'd I was,
So very poor, this was my chance,
Betwixt an ox and a silly poor ass,
To call my true love to my dance.

I SAW THREE SHIPS

I saw three ships come sailing in,
On Christmas Day, on Christmas Day,
I saw three ships come sailing in,
On Christmas Day in the morning.
And what was in those ships all three?
Our Savior Christ and his Lady.

AUSTRIAN HUNTERS' CAROL

Awake, O drowsy hunters,
    Hear the whistles and the horn!
Get up from lazy slumber,
    For our Saviour Christ is born.
From the trumpets' jolly playing
    Let the hills and valleys ring,
Hark, the hunting hounds are baying;
    Go and greet the new-born King!
Awake from sleep, O hunters:
    It is the morn of Christmas day.

SLOVAK CAROL

It was a night in winter,
    Man and beast asleep,
When Jesus, poor and humble,
    Did his vigil keep.
The Lord whom kings and prophets
    Lovingly foretold,
Lies trembling in a stable,
    Dark and bitter cold.
Is this the only welcome,
    Saviour, at your birth?
Is loneliness and sadness
    All you find on earth?

CHRISTMAS HYMNS

Christmas hymns differ from carols
in that the mood of hymns is less playful
and more reflective and meditative.

SILENT NIGHT

Silent night, holy night!
All is calm, all is bright.
'Round yon Virgin Mother and Child,
Holy Infant so tender and mild:
Sleep in heavenly peace,
Sleep in heavenly peace!

Silent night, holy night!
Shepherds quake at the sight!
Glories stream from heaven afar,
Heav'nly hosts sing Alleluia:
Christ, the Savior is born,
Christ, the Savior is born!

O COME ALL YE FAITHFUL

O come, all ye faithful, joyful and triumphant,
O come ye, O come ye to Bethlehem;
Come and behold Him, born, the King of angels;

   O come let us adore Him,
   O come let us adore Him,
   O come let us adore Him, Christ the Lord.

Sing, choirs of angels, sing in exultation,
Sing, all ye citizens of heav'n above;
Glory to God in the highest:

   O come let us adore Him,
   O come let us adore Him,
   O come let us adore Him, Christ the Lord.

HARK!
THE HERALD ANGELS SING

Hark! The herald angels sing,
"Glory to the new-born King,
Peace on earth and mercy mild
God and sinners reconciled."
Joyful all ye nations rise,
Join the triumph of the skies.
With th' angelic host proclaim.
"Christ is born in Bethlehem."

   Hark! The herald angels sing,
   "Glory to the new-born King."

Christ, by highest heaven adored,
Christ, the everlasting Lord.
Late in time behold Him come,
Off-spring of a virgin's womb.
Veiled in flesh, the God-head see;
Hail th' incarnate Deity!
Pleased as Man with men to appear,
Jesus, our Immanuel here!

   Hark! The herald angels sing,
   "Glory to the new-born King."

THE FIRST NOEL

The first Noel the angel did say,
Was to three poor shepherds in fields as they lay;
In fields where they lay keeping their sheep
On a cold winter's night that was so deep.

   Noel, Noel, Noel, Noel,
   Born is the King of Israel.

They looked up and saw a star
Shining in the east, beyond them far,
And to the earth it gave great light,
And so continued both day and night.

   Noel, Noel, Noel, Noel,
   Born is the King of Israel.

PARADISE TREE

Hanging ornaments on trees
seems to go all the way back to Roman times.
Decorating a "Christmas" tree, however,
seems to date from 16th-century Germany.
There, evergreen branches were freighted down
with apples, sugar candy, and painted nuts.

The inspiration for the Christmas tree
came from the "mystery plays,"
performed in churches during the Middle Ages.
A yearly favorite was an Advent performance,
called the "Paradise Play"—man's creation,
expulsion, and the promise of a saviour.

The only prop on stage was a fir tree, with apples
suspended from its branches.
Eventually, the tree found its way into Christian
homes.

Later on, to point out to their children
that the "paradise tree" was no longer a "symbol
of sin," but also a "symbol of salvation,"
16th-century Germans combined it with another
ancient symbol, the "Christmas light."
They also began to hang candy and cookies alongside
the apples of "sin" to symbolize the grace of "salvation."
Thus, the "tree of sin" and the "light of Christ"
grew into the "tree of light," with its
salvation-symbols.
Today we call it the "Christmas tree."

LONDON IMPORT

Prince Albert, the German husband
of Queen Victoria,
introduced the "Christmas tree" to England,
and sweetmeats and wax tapers were added.
Says *The Illustrated London News* for 1848:

"The Christmas Tree is annually prepared
by her Majesty's command
for the Royal children . . .
The tree employed for this festive purpose
is a young fir of about eight feet high,
and has six tiers of branches.
On each tier, or branch, are arranged a dozen
wax tapers . . .
Fancy cakes, gilt gingerbread and
eggs filled with sweetmeats, are suspended
by variously-coloured ribbons
from the branches . . .
On the summit of the tree
stands the small figure of an angel
with outstretched wings,
holding in each hand a wreath."

WINTER GUESTS

Into the house the tree brought with it
the memory of thousands of white-hot summer suns,
the long wilderness of silence of snowmantled winters,
the crash of thunderous storms,
the softness of a new green spring,
and all the wild things
which had rested in its shade or nestled in its branches.

Earl Hamner, Jr.
The Homecoming

40

CROSSING THE OCEAN

During the Revolutionary War,
homesick Hessian troops brought the Christmas tree
to America.
But it was many years before the custom took roots.

"One of the first known trees was set up by
Charles Follen, a German professor at Harvard, in 1832.
Another is credited to August Imgard of Wooster, Ohio,
who as a recent arrival from Germany,
decorated a tree for his nephew and niece in 1847.

Cleveland, Ohio had a tree in 1851,
set up by Pastor Henry Schwan for his congregation.
When some people objected to it as a pagan practice,
the religious character of its origin was explained
and the objections were dropped.

President Franklin Pierce did much to spread
the custom by having a Christmas tree in the
White House (1850's) . . .
President Benjamin Harrison continued the practice
and soon the Christmas tree became an
American tradition.

It was another American president, however,
who almost stopped the custom.
President Theodore Roosevelt,
noted for his efforts in conservation of our natural resources,
banned the Christmas tree tradition at the White House.
His sons, however, smuggled a tree in
and, when confronted with the crime,
were defended by America's first forester, Gifford Pinchot.
Pinchot convinced the president
that the cutting of young evergreens could be helpful
in forest conservation . . ."

Sister Maria Gratia Listaite and Norbert Hildebrand
A New Look at Christmas Decorations

CHRISTMAS GIVING

"The twelfth day of Christmas
My true love sent to me:
Twelve ladies dancing,
Eleven lords a-leaping,
Ten drummers drumming,
Nine pipers piping,
Eight maids a-milking,
Seven swans a-swimming,
Six geese a-laying,
Five gold rings,
Four calling birds,
Three French hens,
Two turtle doves,
And a partridge in a pear tree."

The "12 days of Christmas"
end on January 6th.
Called the
"Feast of the Epiphany,"
this day celebrates
the coming of the
3 wise men,
bearing their gifts
for the newborn king.

PANIC IN A PEAR TREE

Five years ago a young soldier named W.J. Chandler, Jr.
found himself stationed at Fort Bragg just before Christmas
with some time on his hands. He decided to figure out
just what it would cost to send his own true love
all the presents in the song *The Twelve Days of Christmas*.

The figure he arrived at (without comparison shopping)
was $211,758.90. Some items were bargains—
he located drummers right on the post who were willing
to perform for only $50. But the English "calling birds"
came high.

Since the panic over Christmas costs is an annual condition,
even in a pear tree, LIFE ran a check this year for Chandler,
who is now a Charlotte, N.C. attorney. Oddly enough,
in spite of inflation, the total price has gone down a bit.
There are several reasons: we got a better deal
on turtle doves and hens, and some air fares have declined.
But the biggest saving comes from the rate of exchange
between the dollar and the British pound. Since 1967
the pound has dropped about 40 cents, reducing the cost of
the calling birds by $2,506.

Life magazine

THE CANARY

Next morning it was I who waked the whole family
with my first ''Merry Christmas!''
I found surprises, not in the stocking only,
but on the table, on all the chairs, at the door,
on the very window-sill;
indeed, I could hardly walk without stumbling
on a bit of Christmas
wrapped up in tissue paper.
But when my teacher presented me with a canary,
my cup of happiness overflowed.

Helen Keller
The Story of My Life

NO CHRISTMAS

Christmas won't be Christmas
without any presents.

Louisa May Alcott
Little Women

JUST THIS NIGHT

The grinding poverty of the Depression years
had already stamped the older faces
with a gaunt grey pallor,
but the prospect of a gift, of some slight change from
the ordinary, the elusive Christmas Spirit,
had animated thin faces and brought hope to defeated eyes.

Each newcomer joined the group silently,
without any greeting from his neighbor.
They were proud and independent people.
Accepting any kind of outside help went against their grain,
but they had put aside their pride this night
so that their children might receive some token of Christmas
which they themselves were unable to provide.

Earl Hamner, Jr.
The Homecoming

GIFTS IN THE WILDERNESS

[From the *Journal* of explorers Lewis and Clark]
Wednesday, 25 December 1805.

We were awakened at daylight by a discharge
of firearms,
which was followed by a song from the men,
as a compliment to us on the return of Christmas,
which we have always been accustomed to observe
as a day of rejoicing.
After breakfast we divided our remaining stocks of tobacco,
which amounted to twelve carrots, into two parts;
one of which we distributed among such of the party
as made use of it;
making a present of a handkerchief to the others.
The remainder of the day was passed in good spirits,
though there was nothing in our situation to excite
much gaity.

Meriwether Lewis and William Clark
Journal

MEMORIES

It is remembered in my family
that on Christmas Eve of 1933
my father was late arriving home.
That, along with the love he and my mother
bestowed upon their eight red-haired offspring,
is fact.
The rest is fiction.

Earl Hamner, Jr.
The Homecoming

BEGGAR'S RHYME

Christmas is coming,
   the geese are getting fat,
Please to put a penny
   in the old man's hat;
If you haven't got a penny,
   a ha' penny will do.
If you haven't got a ha' penny,
God bless you!

Anonymous

GRANDMA'S GIFT

She had very many friends to love,
    But her purse was very small;
How could she make those few pennies buy
    Enough to gladden all?
So the little face more sober grew,
    The chattering tongue quite still,
Til grandma said, "What's the matter, dear?
    Are you tired or feeling ill?"

Then into grandmother's lap she climbed
    And nested her curly head;
She told her troubles with tearful eyes,
    And this is what Grandma said:

"Love is the very best thing in the world,
    Of that you have given a large store,
You may give and give and give,
    And always have plenty more . . ."

Ruth Davenport
"The Very Best Thing"
in Alice M. Kellogg's
How to Celebrate Thanksgiving and Christmas

AND ST. NICK, TOO . . .

So, up to the house-top the coursers they flew,
With a sleigh full of toys—and St. Nicholas too.
And then in a twinkling I heard on the roof,
The prancing and pawing of each little hoof.

As I drew in my head, and was turning around,
Down the chimney St. Nicholas came with a bound.

Clement C. Moore
"A Visit from St. Nicholas"

DOWN THE CHIMNEY?

In pre-Christian times
the Germans thought of *Hertha*, the Norse goddess,
as the protectress of their homes.
Houses were decked with firs and evergreens
to welcome her.
At the family feast Hertha descended
in the smoke of the burning fir boughs
to her altar stones.

In this ancient story of the Hearth Goddess
may be discerned
the origins of the idea that Santa Claus, of a later age,
must always come down the chimney.
The shoes placed for the Hearth Goddess
eventually became
the stockings hung on the mantel piece.

William H. Crawford, Jr.
Christmas in Germany

49

SINTER KLAAS

St. Nicholas, a popular and kindly bishop,
was imprisoned during the Roman persecutions
of Diocletian in the 4th century.
He was later freed by Constantine.
Today, his body rests in Bari, Italy.

Before and after his death,
numerous miracles were ascribed to the bishop.
As the centuries mounted, St. Nicholas
became a legend in the minds and hearts of
needy Christians.

His feast was celebrated on December 6th,
and its eve became the occasion of gift-giving,
especially to children.
St. Nicholas, himself, supposedly, dispatched
the children's gifts in shoes and stockings.

The name "Santa Claus" derives from "*Sinter Klaas,*"
Holland's modified version of St. Nicholas.
When Dutch settlers came to America, they brought
Sinter Klaas with them.
America, the melting pot of people,
turned out to be the melting pot of traditions, also.
Somehow, Sinter Klaas and England's "Father
Christmas," another gift-giver, went into the same pot
and emerged fused/confused as Santa Claus.
Similarly, the gift-giving night shifted from the eve
of December 5th to the eve of Christ's birth.

TAKING SHAPE

The first American portrait of Santa
was sketched by Thomas Nast in 1850.

"Nast's picture
was a composite of different elements. . .
Saint Nicholas . . . whose Phrygian miter explains
the floppy cap worn by Santa Claus.
To the good bishop was added some of the traits of
Dickens' Ghost of Christmas Past
in *A Christmas Carol* which came out in 1843
and was an instant best-seller in America.
And to compound confusion, Good King Wenceslaus
first looked out in 1853,
in the famous and popular carol of . . .
J. M. Neale.

Joseph Blenkinsopp
"Why Keep On Celebrating Christmas?"
Commonweal

SANTA IN THE ORIENT

In Japan, Santa and Christmas have taken over
by storm.

"Christmas has become so much a part of all
the children of Japan
that many of them are surprised to hear
that the Christian churches also celebrate
Christmas.

The Japanese . . .
take what appeals to them in foreign customs,
but not necessarily their meaning or substance.
Santa Claus was an early victim.
Raised to the rank of deity, he is now equal
to the seven popular gods of good luck.
As a jolly old man,
he reminds the Japanese of someone who has
wined and dined and is ready for plenty of fun.
That is enough to deify him in the Japanese mind,
and that image sets the tone for the
Christmas celebrations . . .

The Japanese family, 'who pray faithfully to their
ancestors before a Buddhist altar . . .
will on Christmas eve
light a colorfully decorated Christmas tree . . .
and join in singing *Silent Night*.' "

The Catholic Digest

JOLLY RED GENT

In Russia, as everywhere else,
the bearer of good tidings this holiday season
is a round and jolly old gent
in high boots and red robe and white whiskers . . .
Santa in his Soviet incarnation is, of course,
a secular saint; his Christianity is conveniently overlooked.
The old gent who comes to reward little Ivan . . .
is known as Grandfather Frost—Dyed Marzo—
and his excuse for making an appearance
is simply the New Year.

Tobi Frankel
"Where Santa Comes by Troika"
McCalls magazine

SANTA CLAUS, INDIANA

This small Disneyland-like hamlet has been
answering "Dear Santa" letters since 1852,
when the local folks,
inspired by the entrance of the village Santa
into a Christmas Eve town meeting,
decided to call the town "Santa Claus."

Santa's mail at the beginning was small in volume
and easily stored in an empty fruit basket in the
general store;
but the Santa Claus postmark today has become
a cherished part of Christmas for some four
million children . . .

Besides the postal business . . .
In the 1930's, an industrious businessman
set up shop in Santa Claus to manufacture
decorative sleighs.
And about the same time, a leading candy company
built a candy castle and from there sold and mailed
candy canes to all parts of the U.S.
(The structure has now been converted into a
gift shop: the St. Nicholas Castle and
Old Curiosity Shop.)

Climaxing the building boom was the dedication
of a forty-ton granite statue of Santa Claus
overlooking what has lately become known as
"Santa's Country."

"Santa's Country"
Holiday magazine

YES, VIRGINIA, THERE IS A SANTA CLAUS

Dear Editor—I am eight years old.
Some of my little friends say there is no
Santa Claus.
Papa says, "If you see it in *The Sun,* it's so."
Please tell me the truth, is there a Santa Claus?

Virginia O'Hanlon
115 West Ninety-fifth Street

Virginia, your little friends are wrong.
They have been affected by the skepticism of a
skeptical age.
They do not believe except what they see.
They think that nothing can be which is not comprehensible
to their little minds . . .

Yes, Virginia, there is a Santa Claus.
He exists as certainly as love and generosity
and devotion exist, and you know that they abound
and give your life its highest beauty and joy.
Alas! how dreary would be the world if there were
no Santa Claus!
It would be as dreary as if there were no Virginias.
There would be no childlike faith then, no poetry,
no romance to make tolerable this existence.
We would have no enjoyment except in sense and sight.
The eternal light with which childhood fills the world
would be extinguished.

Not believe in Santa Claus!
You might as well not believe in fairies! . . .
The most real things in the world are those that
neither children nor men can see.
Did you ever see fairies dancing on the lawn?
Of course not, but that's no proof that they are not there.
Nobody can conceive or imagine all the wonders
there are unseen and unseeable in the world . . .

There is a veil covering the unseen world
which not the strongest man, nor even the united strength
of the strongest men that ever lived can tear apart.
Only faith, fancy, poetry, love, romance
can push aside the curtain and view the picture
the supernal beauty and glory beyond. Is it all real?
Ah Virginia, in all this world there is nothing else
more real . . .

No Santa Claus! Thank God! he lives, and he lives
forever.

Francis P. Church
The Sun, New York City, September 21, 1897

HOLIDAY CANDLES

When religion was suppressed in Ireland during
the English persecution, the people had no churches.
Priests hid in homes to say Mass there during
the night.

Now it was the dearest wish of every Irish family
in those days
that at least once in their lifetimes a priest would
be near their home at Christmas,
so he could come and celebrate the divine sacrifice
during the Holy Night.
For this grace they hoped and prayed all through
the year.

When Christmas came, they left their doors unlocked
and put burning candles in the windows
so that any priest who happened to be in the neighborhood,
would know that he was expected and welcomed.
The light of the candles guided him to the house. . .
Their home was to be a church during the Holy Night.

The English soldiers, being suspicious of such customs,
asked the Irish what the purpose . . . was . . .

"We burn the candles and keep the doors unlocked
that Mary and Joseph, looking for a place to stay,
will find their way to our home and be welcomed with
open hearts."

The English authorities finding this Irish "superstition"
harmless, did not bother to suppress it.

Francis X. Weiser
The Year of Our Lord in the Christian Home

CHRISTMAS DOWN-UNDER

. And so it's Christmas in the South
    as on the North Seacoasts,
Though we are starv'd with summer-drouth,
    and you with winter frosts.
And we shall have our roast beef here
    and think of you the while,
Though all the watery hemisphere
    cuts off the mother isle.

Feel sure that we think of you,
    we who have wandered forth;
And many a million thoughts
    will go today from south to north;
Old heads will muse on churches old,
    where bells will ring today—
The very bells perchance which tolled
    their fathers to the clay.

And now good-night and I shall dream
    that I am with you all,
Watching the ruddy embers gleam
    athwart the panelled hall;
Nor care I if I dream or not,
    though severed by the foam,
My heart is always in the spot
    which was my childhood's home.

Douglas B. W. Sladen
"Christmas Letter from Australia"
In F. Cusack's
The Australian Christmas

KING OLAF'S CHRISTMAS

At Drontheim, Olaf the King
Heard the bells of Yule-tide ring,
As he sat in his banquet-hall,
Drinking the nut-brown ale,
With his bearded Berserks hale
and tall.

O'er his drinking horn, the Sign
He made of the Cross divine
As he drank, and muttered his prayers,
But the Berserks ever more
Made the sign of the Hammar of Thor
Over theirs.

Henry Wadsworth Longfellow
"King Olaf's Christmas"

A WELSH CHRISTMAS

The traditional *Hodening Horse* may still be found
wandering about the streets of remote Welsh villages.
This horse is a frightful creature
with a carved wooden head,
and two boys and a sheet for a body.
The head is as grotesque as possible
and is often painted in outlandish colors.
Sometimes the mouth and eyes are dug out,
and the candle placed behind them
gives the effect of flame and smoke belching out
in the manner of the dragons of olden days.

All this is designed to scare the inmates of the houses
out of their wits and to encourage them
to placate the Hodening Horse with refreshments of
cake and cider.
Often, the Horse recites long extemporaneous poems,
to which the host must reply *ex tempore*
and in equal length.
Hodening Horse, naturally, outwits the host
and gains admittance to the house.
Once the ritual of the Hodening Horse is over
and the callers have had their rewards of sweets, cakes,
picks (cookies), or ale,
the company will sing some Christmas songs.

William H. Crawford
Holidays in Wales

A-WASSAILING

After the yule log is lighted,
the fireplace becomes the focal point
for most of the Christmas activities
with guests making merry by drinking wassail
and singing carols.
The wassail bowl is first paraded around the room
and then set in front of the fire,
where it is kept warm.

Wassail Song

"Wassail, wassail, all over town;
Our bread it is white and our ale—it is brown.
Our bowl, it is made of the white maple tree;
With the wassailing bowl we will drink unto thee.

Then here's to the horse, and to his right eye!
May God send our master a good Christmas pie,
A good Christmas Pie that may we all see!
With the wassailing bowl we'll drink unto Thee!"

Marguerite Ickis
The Book of Christmas

Wassail, which is perhaps the best known of
Christmas drinks, originated with the Anglo-Saxons.
The word derives from *wes hal*, meaning
"be in health."

In 18th century England,
the well-to-do sat around large tables
and passed from hand to hand
the wassail bowl with its delicious aroma,
floating nut meats and bits of toast,
wishing one another good health.
The poorer people would take mugs
bedecked with ribbons and go "a-wassailing"
from door to door, asking for money to buy
a bit of brew
so they too could regale themselves.

The Life Book of Christmas, Volume Three
The Merriment of Christmas
courtesy Time-Life Books

TOUCH HANDS

Ah friends, dear friends, as years go on
    and heads get gray, how fast the guests do go!
Touch hands, touch hands, with those that stay.
Strong hands to weak, old hands to young,
    around the Christmas board, touch hands.
The false forget, the foe forgive,
    for every guest will go and every fire burn low
    and cabin empty stand.
Forget, forgive, for who may say that Christmas day
    may ever come to host or guest again.
Touch hands!

William H. H. Murray
"John Norton's Vagabond"

WHISTLE ON

Heap on more wood!—
The wind is chill;
But let it whistle as it will,
We'll keep our Christmas merry still.
Each age has deemed the new-born year
The fittest time for festal cheer . . .

"Sir Walter Scott
Marmion"

TO THE FIRING

The ancient yule log ceremony is a
favorite Christmas celebration in our northern states.
The choppers meet on the village square,
and after a round of carol singing,
they head for the woods to search for the Yule log,
which was notched and hidden there weeks before.
The discoverers haul it to its destination
with great pomp and ceremony,
where it is lighted with a brand saved from
the year before.
The log is highly decorated with greens and bright
colored ribbons
and the youngest child rides atop
as it is being hauled from the woods.

Among ceremonies used for lighting the yule log
is one in which the youngest child in the home
pours wine on the log while the father
offers a prayer that the fire might warm the cold,
that the hungry might gain food,
that the weary find rest, and
that all enjoy heaven's peace.

Another moving ceremony is one
where all guests are assembled and as
the yule log approaches
the entire company begins to sing the old song
written by Robert Herrick:

"Come bring, with a noise,
My merrie, merrie boys
The Christmas log to the firing . . ."

Then the host rises and holding high his cup,
he shouts . . .
"This yule log burns.
It destroys all hatreds and misunderstandings.
Let your envies banish,
and let the spirit of good fellowship reign supreme
for this season through all the year."

Marguerite Ickis
The Book of Christmas

A RUDDY BLAZE

The yule log
"is a great log of wood, sometimes the root
of a tree, brought into the house with great
ceremony, on Christmas Eve,
laid in the fireplace and lighted . . .

While it lasted, there was great drinking,
singing, and telling of tales.
Sometimes it was accompanied by Christmas candles;
but in the cottages the only light was from
the ruddy blaze of the great wood fire. . .
Herrick mentions it in one of his songs—

'Come, bring with a noise
My merrie, merrie boyes,
The Christmas log to the firing;
While my good dame, she
Bids ye all be free,
And drink to your heart's desiring.'"

Washington Irving
Christmas Papers

61

CHRISTMAS DINNER

The Christmas Table was so long
and there were so many of us,
that a few of the chairs were caught in a jog
of the wall and had no proper approach
except by crawling on hands and knees beneath it. . .

The dinner itself was a prodigious feast.
The cookstove must have rested and panted
for a week thereafter.

Before long, Annie got so red
bringing in turkeys and cranberry sauce . . .
that one might think she herself
was in the process to become a pickled beet
and would presently enter on a platter.

Charles S. Brooks
Chimney-Pot Papers

CHRISTMAS DISHES

France:	Potage Noel
Lebanon:	Lamb Soup
Italy:	Tortellini in Brodo
Sweden:	Rice Porridge
Poland:	Stuffed Carp
Spain:	Shrimp Casserole

Henry VIII's chef baked a Christmas plum pie
which used 2 bushels of flour,
24 pounds of butter, and 8 varieties of meat.
It weighed 165 pounds, was 9 feet long,
and had to be wheeled to the table on a cart.

As many mince pies as you taste
at Christmas
so many happy months will you have.

Old English Saying

FROM OUR HOUSE
TO YOUR HOUSE

Card collectors still rummage dusty attics
hoping to find an early "Prang."
One hundred years ago, Louis Prang of Boston
put on sale America's first Christmas cards.

Though collectors cherish the "Prangs,"
many a busy housewife wishes he would have
stuck to wall prints.
Actually, the blame/credit isn't Prang's.
He merely started doing what had been going on
in England for almost 20 years.

It seems that the first engraved Christmas card
showed up in London in 1842,
but the idea didn't become popular for another
20 years or so.
Now, over 5 billion cards a year bulge from
the postman's bag each December.

Somewhat related to the mailing of Christmas cards
to friends is the practice of writing letters to Santa.
Though American children send their letters to
Santa at the North Pole,
Bavarian children send simple notes to "Jesus."
They deposit them, not in mailboxes, but on the
window sill, sometime before St. Nicholas makes
his rounds during the night of December 5th.

PERSONAL EXPRESSION

The newest thing on the market
is do-it-yourself cards;
the customer can put together his own missive
by selecting one of a variety of illustrations
and then matching it
with any of several messages. . .

The genius of the greeting-card industry
is probably the way it has legitimized sentimentality.
We needn't be embarrassed about emotion;
if it's printed, it leaves that certain distance,
which provides space enough for the
unsentimental image and the sentimental reality
to coexist comfortably.

"About This Issue"
Harper's magazine

EPSTEIN,
SPARE THAT YULE LOG!

Oh, give me an old-fashioned Christmas card
With hostlers hostling in an old inn yard,
With church bells chiming their silver notes,
And jolly red squires in their jolly red coats,
And a good fat goose by the fire that dangles,
And a few more angels and a few less angles.
Turn backward, time, to please this bard
And give me an old-fashioned Christmas card.

Ogden Nash
"Epstein, Spare that Yule Log!"

LEGEND
OF THE FLOWER

The poinsettia
was named after Dr. Joel Roberts Poinsett . . .
who served as United States Ambassador to Mexico.
Upon his return in 1829, he brought this flower
with him to his home in South Carolina,
where it flourished.

The people of Mexico call the poinsettia
the "flower of the Holy Night."
A charming Mexican legend explains its origin:
On a Christmas eve, long ago, a poor little boy
went to church in great sadness, because he
had no gift to bring the Holy Child.
He dared not enter the church, and,
kneeling humbly on the ground outside the
house of God, he prayed fervently and assured our Lord,
with tears, how much he desired to offer Him
some lovely present—
"But I am very poor and dread to approach You
with empty hands."
When he finally rose from his knees, he saw
springing up at his feet a green plant
with gorgeous blooms of dazzling red.

Francis X. Weiser
The Christmas Book

"MAGIC" MISTLETOE

. . . Cutting of the mistletoe
was an occasion of great solemnity.
The Druid priests
headed a stately procession into the forest.
When the chosen oak tree was reached,
the Arch-Druid, robed all in white, climbed the tree
and cut down the sacred vine with a golden sickle.
Falling to earth,
the mistletoe was caught in a fair cloth,
spread out for the purpose by immaculate maidens.
Then it was divided, and each family
bore home a sprig to hang over the door;
for it was believed that the powers of the plant
to cure and to protect were very great.
The English
called the mistletoe 'allheal', the Welsh, *guidhel.*
"If one hangs mistletoe about the neck,
the witches can have no power over him."

William H. Crawford
Holidays in Wales

DIVINE HEALER

The "magic" plant of the mistletoe,
called "all heal" by the pagan Druids,
was used in Christian times as a symbol of Christ,
the Divine Healer of all nations.

Francis X. Weiser
The Year of Our Lord in the Christian Home

"The mistletoe bough at our Christmas board
Shall hang, to honor Christ the Lord:
For He is the evergreen tree of Life. . ."

quoted by Francis X. Weiser
in *The Year of Our Lord in the Christian Home*

"What this planet needs
is more mistletoe
and less missile-talk."

Wall Graffiti

THE HOLLY AND THE IVY

The holly bears a berry,
As red as any blood,
And Mary bore sweet Jesus Christ
To do poor sinners good:

The holly bears a prickle,
As sharp as any thorn,
And Mary bore sweet Jesus Christ
On Christmas day in the morn:

The holly bears a bark,
As bitter as any gall,
And Mary bore sweet Jesus Christ
For to redeem us all . . .

16th Century Carol

3

His Day

A TIME OF FULFILLMENT

WHEN THE WORLD WAS AT PEACE

In the year
5199 from the creation of the world,
from the beginning when God created heaven
and earth—

2957 from the flood—

2015 from the birth of Abraham—

1510 from Moses and the coming of the
Israelites out of Egypt—

and from King David's annointing, 1032;

in the 65th week of the prophecy of Daniel;

in the year 752 from the founding of the
City of Rome;

in the 42nd year of the empire of Octavian Augustus,
when the whole world was at peace,

in the 6th age of the world,

Jesus Christ, eternal God and Son of the eternal
Father,
desiring to redeem the world by his merciful coming,

having been conceived by the Holy Spirit
and nine months having passed since his conception,

Is born in Bethlehem of Judea,
having become man of the Virgin Mary.

Christmas Reading
Roman Martyrology

PAX ROMANA

"At that time
Emperor Augustus sent out an order
for all citizens of the Empire
to register themselves for the census . . .
each to his own land."

Luke 2: 1–3

It was an appropriate time for a census;
the entire Roman-controlled world
was at peace.
Augustus Caesar,
"the author of the *pax romana*,
had reached the peak of his pyramid of glory. . .
He was given honors
hitherto unknown in the empire;
temples and entire cities were dedicated to him,
and he was proclaimed to be
of divine, not human, origin."

Giuseppe Ricciotti
The Life of Christ

PROPHECY

But in Palestine,
a tiny, out-of-the-way slice of the Roman empire,
there were problems:

"The Jews—'stiff-necked people'—
bore the Roman yoke with smoldering hatred.
Self-proclaimed Messiahs,
revolutionaries, false prophets arose.
Everywhere
they and their followers were brutally crushed.

Brigands and guerillas infested the hills.
Fanatical Jewish rebels called Zealots
spread terror with their concealed daggers.
Tax collectors squeezed the peasantry
while Roman-appointed monarchs—
Herod the Great and his sons—
lived in pagan splendor.
Many Jews foresaw 'the end of days'
and coming of the Messiah,
the anointed one promised by the prophets.
He would restore Israel's glory."

Howard LaFay
"The Years in Galilee"
in the National Geographic Society's
Everyday Life in Bible Times

PREPARE THE WAY

More than ever, Jews began to ponder
the words of the prophet, Isaiah:

"A shoot shall sprout from the stump of Jesse,
and from his roots a bud shall blossom.
The spirit of the Lord shall rest upon him:
a spirit of wisdom and of understanding,
A spirit of counsel and of strength,
a spirit of knowledge and of fear of the Lord. . .

Not by appearance shall he judge,
nor by hearsay shall he decide,
But he shall judge the poor with justice,
and decide aright for the land's afflicted. . .

Then the wolf shall be a guest of the lamb,
and the leopard shall lie down with the kid;
The calf and the young lion shall browse together,
with a little child to guide them. (11:1-6)

The Lord himself will give you this sign:
the virgin shall be with child, and bear a son,
and shall name him Immanuel. (7:14)

Prepare the way of the Lord!
Make straight in the desert a highway for our God . . .
Go up unto the high mountain . . . cry out . . .
Here is your God!" (40:3-9)

THE PROMISE
OF TOMORROW MORNING

To a Jew the 'coming' of the Messiah
". . . was a sweet national obsession.
It was ecstasy beyond happiness,
joy beyond comprehension;
it was balm to the weary farmer's bones
as he lay with his family
waiting for sleep;
it was the single last hope of the aged,
the thing a child
looked to a mountain of moving clouds to see;
it was the hope of Judea in chains;
the Messiah was always the promise
of tomorrow morning."

Jim Bishop
The Day Christ Died

DOES SOMEONE HEAR?

The hopes
that lost in some far-distance seem,
may be the truer life
and this the dream

Adelaid Procter
"A Legend of Provence"

So runs my dream:
but what am I
An infant crying in the night:
An infant crying for the light:
And with no language but a cry.

Alfred, Lord Tennyson
"Oh Yet We Trust"

76

. . . AND SOMEONE DID HEAR!

"God sent the Angel Gabriel
to a town in Galilee named Nazareth."
Luke 1: 26

How strange Nazareth!
This hill village was regarded as a 'hicktown'
by many of its biblical contemporaries.
Later, when Nathaniel was told
that the Messiah had come from here,
he snorted sarcastically:
"What good can come out of Nazareth?"
(John 1:46)

Today, parts of Nazareth still resemble
ancient Nazareth.
Hawking peddlers still prod tiny pack-laden donkeys,
and merchants still hustle passers-by
from booths.
The air rings with haggling,
and smells with sweet fruit, olives, spices,
and freshly baked bread.
New-killed lambs dangle from butcher's hooks,
and children eye honey-coated pastries.

THE MAIDEN, MARY

To Nazareth, God sent the Angel Gabriel.

"He had a message for a girl
promised in marriage to a man named Joseph . .
The girl's name was Mary."

Luke 1: 27

"Mary probably was no more than
14 when she bore Jesus.
In her daily rounds, she would have
fetched water, tended the fire, and
ground grain.
The family dined on porridge of wheat
or barley groats . . .
supplemented by beans, lentils, cucumbers,
and other vegetables . . .

For dessert came dates, figs, pomegranates.
Watered wine was the universal drink.
Only on feast days
did humble Galileans eat meat."

Howard LaFay
"The Years in Galilee"
in The National Geographic Society's
Everyday Life in Bible Times

Today, Nazareth claims one unquestionable link
to biblical Nazareth.
The mother of Jesus
certainly drew water at 'Mary's Well;'
there is no other well in modern Nazareth.

MAY MY SPIRIT DARE?

The praises of the young maid, Mary,
have been sung through the ages.
And some of the praises have come from
the most unlikely poets.

"In joy and wo—in good and ill—
Mother of God, be with me still!"

Edgar Allan Poe
"Hymn"

"Woman! above all women glorified
Our tainted nature's solitary boast;
Purer than foam on central ocean tost;
Brighter than eastern skies at daybreak strewn"

William Wordsworth
"The Virgin"

"Ave Maria! may our spirits dare
Look up to thine and to thy Son's above!"

George Gordon, Lord Byron
"Don Juan"

SONG OF AN "UN-POET"

Outside Grand Central Station
a shoe-shine boy was shining shoes.
As he whipped his shine-cloth, again and again,
over his customer's shoes,
a silver medal danced about on his neck.

"Sonny," asked a big man, smoking a cigar,
"What's the hardware around your neck?"

"It's a medal of Mary, the mother of Jesus,"
the boy answered.

"But, why her medal?" asked the man.
"She's no different, kid,
from your own mother."

"That's right, Mister," answered the boy,
"but there's a hell of a difference
between her son and me."

The big man took a puff from his cigar,
flipped the boy a quarter and walked on.

HOW CAN THIS BE?

The Angel Gabriel said to Mary:

"Peace be with you!
The Lord is with you, and has greatly blessed you!"

Mary was deeply troubled by the angel's message,
and she wondered what his words meant.

The angel said to her:

"Don't be afraid, Mary, for God has been
gracious to you.
You will become pregnant and give birth to a son,
and you will name him Jesus . . ."

Mary said to the angel, "I am a virgin.
How can this be?" (Luke 1:31-34)

BY THE GRACE OF GOD

O happy Virgin,
open your heart to faith,
open your lips to consent,
open your bosom to your Creator.
Behold the desired of all nations
is standing outside and knocking at your door . . .

Arise, therefore,
and make haste to open to him . . .

And Mary said,
"Behold the handmaid of the Lord,
be it done to me
according to your word." (Luke 1:38)

*St. Bernard's Sermons for the Seasons
and Principal Feasts of the Year*

GO
TELL IT
ON THE MOUNTAIN

Go tell it on the mountain
Over the hills and everywhere
Go tell it on the mountain,
Our Jesus Christ is born.

When I was a learner,
I sought both night and day;
I asked the Lord to help me,
And he showed me the way.

Go tell it on the mountain
Over the hills and everywhere,
God tell it on the mountain,
Our Jesus Christ is born.

American Spiritual

NO MAN
IS A STRANGER

Mary's answer changes human history.
Jesus now enters the family of man.

In his gospel account of Jesus' birth,
Luke includes a family tree of Jesus' ancestry.
Writing mainly for non-Jews,
Luke's purpose is theological, not biographical.
This becomes clear when we contrast
Luke's geneology with Matthew's.

Matthew begins with Abraham
and moves forward to Jesus.
Luke, however, begins with Jesus
and moves backward—all the way to Adam.

Matthew, writing mainly for Jews,
wants to affirm Jesus' bond with Abraham,
the father of Israel.
Luke, on the other hand, wants to
affirm Jesus' bond with the entire human family.
He wants to stress for his non-Jewish readers
that Jesus' mission is to all men, not just to Israel.

BETHLEHEM

So it happened that
"Joseph went from the town of Nazareth . . .
to register himself with Mary . . .
She was pregnant,
and while they were in Bethlehem,
the time came for her to have her baby." (Luke 2: 1-6)

NEWS ITEM

BETHLEHEM, Occupied Jordan, Dec. 25 [AP]—
Shepherds watched their flocks by night and armed
Israeli troops patrolled the hills around Bethlehem today
as Christmas came to the town where Jesus was born.

Israeli security forces kept a night watch over the
hilltop town in case of Arab guerrilla sabotage
as Christmas began with midnight mass in the
incense-laden grotto, where tradition says the manger
of Jesus lay on the first Christmas.

Bells pealed from the Crusader-built Church of the
Nativity and Christmas reached a climax
with a Roman Catholic pontifical high mass. . . .

Outside, Arab Christians from Bethlehem
and the few foreign tourists who defied Middle East
tension to come to the Holy Land,
watched the proceedings on a giant television screen
affixed to the wall of Bethlehem's police station. . . .

Associated Press
December 25, 1973

CELEBRATING IN BETHLEHEM

In Bethlehem three different rites of Christmas
are celebrated at different times.
First comes the celebration by the Churches of the
Western world that follow the "new"
Gregorian calendar,
introduced in the 16th century.
Then, 12 days later,
just when we are celebrating Epiphany,
the Christmas rite of the Eastern Orthodox Church,
which still follows the old Julian calendar, begins.
Finally, 12 days after that
comes the celebration of the Armenian Church,
whose followers still uphold the earliest tradition
of the coincidence of Christmas,
the day of Christ's birth,
with Epiphany, the day of his baptism 30 years later.

Margaret Mead
"Christmas in Other Lands"
Redbook magazine

HOUSE OF BREAD

Ancient Bethlehem
was a bustling crossroads for commercial caravans.
After dwindling to a handful of inhabitants
in the 16th century, modern Bethlehem has become
a thriving tourist center.
Hardly a day passes without buses unloading tourists
at the door of the oldest, active church in Christendom.

St. Jerome reports that in 135 A.D. the Emperor
Hadrian desecrated the cave in which Jesus was
believed to have been born.

Over the spot, he placed a pagan shrine.
Ironically, this shrine helped to mark the spot
so that 2 centuries later Constantine could erect
a Christian church over the site.

Around 550, the Emperor Justinian enlarged the
Church of the Nativity. It still stands today.

Thus it happened that Jesus,
who later called himself
the "bread of life" (John 6:35)
was to be born in Bethlehem,
which means the "house of bread."

NO ROOM

The hour came.

Mary gave birth to her firstborn son,
wrapped him in clothes
and laid him in a manger—
there was no room for them to stay in the inn.

Luke 2: 7

Welcome all wonders in one sight!
    Eternity shut in span!
Summer in Winter, Day in Night!
    Heaven in Earth, and God in Man!
Great little One! whose all-embracing birth
Lifts Earth to Heaven, stoops Heaven to Earth . . .

To Thee, meek Majesty! soft king
    Of simple graces and sweet Loves:
Each of us his lamb will bring,
    Each his pair of silver doves:
Till burnt at last in fire of Thy eyes,
Ourselves become our own best sacrifice!

Richard Crashaw
"The Shepherds' Hymn"

PARADOX

He who feeds the hungry million birds
Himself hungers for His mother's milk.
The unbeginning God
is born anew in time;
The Ancient of the days
is but an hour old.
He is the everlasting Man . . .
God the Giver and God the Gift
lies cradled in hay
before our shining eyes.

Bernard Wuellner
The Graces of Christmas

PRAYER

I'm sure that Mary longed for warm, sweet words
That lonely night she came to Bethlehem
And there are those around me now, I think,
Who seek the inn. Oh, help me comfort them!

Helen Louise Welshimer
"Prayer for Direction"
in R. M. Elmquist's
50 Years of Christmas

PEACE ON EARTH

There were some shepherds . . .
who were spending the night in the fields,
taking care of their flocks.
An angel of the Lord appeared to them,
and the glory of the Lord shone over them.
They were terribly afraid,
but the angel said to them:

"Don't be afraid!
For I am here with good news for you,
which will bring joy to all the people.
This very night in David's town
your Savior was born—Christ the Lord! . . ."

Suddenly a great army of heaven's angels
appeared with the angel, singing praises to God:
"Glory to God in the highest heaven!
And peace on earth to men
with whom He is pleased!" (Luke 2:8-14)

If we were to go to Bethlehem today
and look down from the sun baked ridge
of the Judean plateau,
we would see a plot of uncultivated land,
and very likely a few shepherds seeking shelter
from the sun
in the shadow of some old and gnarled olive trees.
Possibly, too, we might catch a glimpse
of a flock of broad-tailed, long-eared sheep
nibbling at the close-cropped grass.

Roger Mercurio
"The Shepherds at the Crib—
A Lucan Vignette"
The Bible Today

Biblical shepherds . . .
were tough characters
who promptly and fearlessly used their clubs
to bash in the heads of wolves
that came bothering their flocks,
and they would not have hesitated to do the same
for the Scribes and Pharisees
who came bothering their consciences.
Hence these despised and pugnacious rustics
were excluded from the law courts . . .

Giuseppe Ricciotti
The Life of Christ

LYING IN A MANGER

When the angels went away . . .
the shepherds said to one another,
"Let us go to Bethlehem and see this thing
that has happened . . ."
So they hurried off and found Mary and Joseph,
and saw the baby lying in the manger.

Luke 2: 15–16

The stable which Mary and Joseph found
was probably already partially occupied by animals;
it may have been dark and filthy with dung,
but it was somewhat removed from the village and
therefore quiet and private, and that was enough . . .

Giuseppe Ricciotti
The Life of Christ

STARRY STRANGER

We saw Thee in Thy balmy nest,
    Young dawn of our eternal Day;
We saw Thine eyes break from their East,
    And chase the trembling shades away:
We saw Thee: and we blessed the sight,
We saw Thee by Thine own sweet light.

Poor world, said I, what wilt thou do
    To entertain this starry Stranger?
Is this the best thou canst bestow—
    A cold and not too cleanly manger?
Contend, the powers of Heaven and Earth,
To fit a bed for this huge birth.

Proud world, said I, cease your contest,
    And let the mighty babe alone;
The phoenix builds the phoenix nest,
    Love's architecture is his own.
The babe whose birth embraves this morn,
Made His own bed ere he was born . . .

Richard Crashaw
"The Shepherds' Hymn"

A CHRISTMAS BALLAD

[From the flyleaf of an Edward VI
prayerbook, 1549]

The Storke she rose on Christmas Eve
And sayed unto her broode,
I now must fare to Bethlehem
To view the sonne of God.

She gave to eche his doe of mete,
She stowed them fayrlie in,
And faire she flew and fast she flew,
And came to Bethlehem.

Now where is He of David's line?
She asked at House and Halle,
He is not here, they spake hardlye,
But in the maungier stalle.

She found Him in the maungier stalle
With that most Hoyle Mayde;
The gentyle storke she wept to see
The Lord so rudelye layde.

Then from her panntynge brest she plucked
The feathers whyte and warm;
She strawed them in the maungier bed
To keep the Lord from harm.

Now blessed bee the gentyle Storke
Forever more quothe hee,
For that she saw My saddle estate,
And showed Pytye.

Full welcome shall shee ever bee
In hamlet and in halle,
And night (called) henceforth the Blessed Byrd
And friend of babyes all.

Marguerite Ickis
The Book of Christmas

PRAYER
OF A ROMAN SOLDIER
ON CHRISTMAS EVE

My name is Marcus, and I'm praying, God,
Because it's been so long since I have trod
Upon the hills beside the walls of Rome,
The lovely city that was once My Home.
To see my tender wife, look in her eyes,
And feel her hold me close and hear her sighs
Of Love. My God, why can't I go there now?

It's been a painful time since I have prayed.
Not since the days when thoughtlessly I played
Along the streets that curled around my home.
The center of the world, and yet My Rome . . .

I offer prayers and incense now, O God,
To ask why I must spend this time abroad,
To guard this cold and lonely land today,
Leaving my sweet wife so far away.

The stars I'm watching shine upon her too,
Except they seldom shine the way they do
Right now above that little stable there.
I've never seen such brightness anywhere,
Not even in the brightest pyres of Rome.
O God, O God, how much I miss my home! . . .

Nick Iuppa
"Prayer of a Roman Soldier
On Christmas Eve"
Sign magazine

MEN FROM THE EAST

Soon afterwards some men who studied the
stars came from the east to Jerusalem and
asked:
"Where is the baby born to be the king of the Jews?
We saw his star when it came up in the east,
and we have come to worship him."

When King Herod heard about this he was very
upset, and so was everybody else in Jerusalem.
He called together all the chief priests
and the teachers of the Law and asked them,
"Where will the Messiah be born?"
"In the town of Bethlehem, in Judea," they answered
"This is what the prophet wrote:

'You, Bethelehem, in the land of Judah,
Are not by any means the least among the
rulers of Judah;
For from you will come a leader
Who will guide my people Israel.' ' '

So Herod called the visitors from the east to a
secret meeting and found out from them
the exact time the star had appeared.
Then he sent them to Bethlehem
with these instructions:
"Go and make a careful search for the child
and when you find him let me know,
so that I may go and worship him too."

With this they left, and on their way they saw
the star—the same one they had seen in the east—
and it went ahead of them until it came and stopped
over the place where the child was . . .
They . . . saw the child with his mother Mary . . .
and worshipped him;
then they opened their bags and offered him presents:
gold, frankincense, and myrrh.

God warned them in a dream not to go back to Herod;
so they went back home by another road.

Matthew 2: 1–12

SPACESHIP FOR JESUS

What of the star which led the Magi to Bethlehem?
Some have suggested that it may have been
Halley's comet which crosses the sky every
seventy-six years . . .
Kepler was convinced, however, that what the Magi
saw was the conjunction in the Sign of the Fish of the
planets Venus, Jupiter and Saturn.
This phenomenon . . . happens only at intervals of
seven hundred and ninety-four years.
Kepler himself saw it and defended his hypothesis
in a best-seller of 1606 entitled *De Stella Nova*.
There are also references to it in ancient Chinese
writings and among the Babylonians who were able,
apparently, to predict it in advance . . .

Perhaps the most original suggestion is that of
Immanuel Velikovsky, author of *Worlds in Collision*.
He seems to believe that what the Magi saw
was a spaceship bringing Jesus,
an extraterrestrial being, to this planet.

Joseph Blenkinsopp
"Why Keep On Celebrating Christmas?"
Commonweal magazine

STAR OF THE NATIVITY

And, shyer than a watchman's light,
One star alone
Unseen until then
Shone bright on the way to Bethlehem.

Attributed to Doctor Zhivago
by Boris Basternak
"Star of the Nativity"

TO EGYPT

After the Magi had left, an angel of the Lord
appeared in a dream to Joseph and said:
"Get up, take the child and his mother and run
away to Egypt,
and stay there until I tell you to leave.
Herod will be looking for the child to kill him."

So Joseph got up, took the child and his mother,
and left during the night for Egypt,
where he stayed until Herod died.

Matthew 2: 13–15

NIGHTMARE AND DREAM

When Herod realized that the visitors from
the east had tricked him, he was furious.
He gave orders to kill all the boys in Bethlehem
and its neighborhood who were two years and
younger . . .

Matthew 2: 16

After Herod had died, an angel of the Lord
appeared in a dream to Joseph in Egypt . . .
So Joseph got up, took the child and his mother,
and went back to the country of Israel . . .

He made his home in a town named Nazareth.

Matthew 2: 19–23

RING OUT, RING IN

Ring out, wild bells, to the wild sky,
   the flying cloud, the frosty light:
   the year is dying in the night;
Ring out, wild bells, and let him die. . . .

Ring out the want, the care, the sin,
   the faithless coldness of the times;
   Ring out, ring out mournful rhymes,
But ring the fuller minstrel in . . .

Ring in the valiant man and free,
   the larger heart, the kindlier hand;
   Ring out the darkness of the land,
Ring in the Christ that is to be.

Alfred, Lord Tennyson
"Christmas and New Year's Bells"

4

Tomorrow

A DECISION

WHAT IF

Still . . .
Jesus was crazy.

He came into the world with the nutty idea that
human beings could love one another. . . .

Peace on earth indeed.
Maybe Jesus should have stayed home.
He was wrong. We cannot love one another.
The best we can do is keep the levels of hatred
low enough so we don't exterminate one another
before we all die of pollution or the world gets
fouled up in the ultimate rush hour traffic jam. . . .

It was a great idea, of course.
Too bad it didn't work. . . .

Still . . .

What if He wasn't crazy? What if He was right?
What if it is possible to love one another?
What if the lion can lie down with the lamb?
What if Arab and Jew, Protestant and Catholic,
black and white, young and old, male and female
can love one another without fear, without hatred,
without death and destruction? . . .

What if the crib scene is what the world is really
all about and everything else is phony?
What would it be like if Jesus knew the way things
really were?
What if life does triumph over death, light over
darkness, good over evil, love over hate,
comedy over tragedy?

Andrew Greeley
"Christmas really is a humbug"
Chicago Tribune

NO WINE FOR ROBOTS

Although the office Christmas party has
acquired a bad reputation for encouraging boozing
and illegitimate flirtations,
these are side effects of something basically good—
the realization that co-workers are not merely
robots cranking out sales orders, typed letters
and balanced ledger pages endlessly.

Robots can be lined up and turned off
when not in use,
and there'll never be any trouble.
When human beings are assembled in one place,
excitement of some kind is more than likely.
Nevertheless, it's better to be human than a robot.
("Son, they have no wine.")

Richard Frisbie
"Let's Keep the Tinsel in Christmas"
U.S. Catholic

We love all which tends to call man from the
solitary and chilling pursuit of his own separate and
selfish views,
into the warmth of common sympathy,
and within the bands of a common brotherhood.

Marguerite Ickis
The Book of Christmas

ROOM FOR RUDOLPH

Even if we don't like
mechanical Santa Clauses howling out, "Ho, Ho, Ho"
and Christmas carols
roaring out of a loud speaker in a shopping center,
can't we still rejoice . . .?

James A. Dunn
"Sounding Board"
U.S. Catholic

I feel that Santa, Rudolph, and Mr. Scrooge
belong in Christmas.

We have the unlucky facility of growing up
too fast; we have very little childhood any more.
We force our children
to grow up before they leave the 7th grade. I feel
that Christmas with its tinsel makes us children again.

Martin J. Kenny, Jr.
"Sounding Board"
U.S. Catholic

SOLDIER'S CHRISTMAS:
Valley Forge General Hospital
in Pennsylvania

If a man is well enough to travel, he's sent home
on a Christmas leave;
if he's not up to the journey, his family is given
an opportunity to visit him.
From as far away as Hawaii, they are flown in,
all expenses paid,
for a three day Christmas reunion . . .

The patient is usually bewildered, unbelieving,
thunderstruck. Somebody is doing this for *him*?
The conversation might go something like this:

"We're flying your mother and father in from
California . . ."

"You're *what*? But they can't afford to . . ."

"Everything's paid for—plane, motel, taxis, meals . . ."

"You're kidding. *Who's* paying?"

"Oh, people around Philadelphia who want to say thanks
for what you've done. A lot of people have given money."

"Wow! Who says there's no Santa Claus?!!"

Catherine Lanham Miller
"Hospital Christmas"
Good Housekeeping magazine

REACHING OUT

Admittedly, Christmastime is traumatic.
People are badgered by merchants . . .
And this is the moment when the charitable organizations
come around to ask for contributions.
It seems poor timing . . .
But the charities have found Christmas to be
a good season to raise funds.
Despite everything, people are in a generous mood.

Upon examination, the much-criticized American way
of Christmas turns out to be basically an occasion
for doing something for others
and reaching out to renew human contacts.

Richard Frisbie
"Let's Keep the Tinsel in Christmas"
U.S. Catholic

Christmas is
"the only time I know of,
in the long calendar of the year
when men and women seem by one consent
to open their shut-in hearts freely."

Charles Dickens
A Christmas Carol

DREAM MAGIC

The magic of Christmas
is a powerful magic indeed . . .
Christmas magic reunites scattered families,
causes perfect strangers to greet one another . . .
Now is the time when children reveal
their impossible desires.
Little girls are not afraid to ask for ponies;
little boys dream of space ships that will really fly to
the moon.
Even sensible adults are caught up in the spirit of
what-might-be . . .

So the sense of excitement grows
until Christmas morning dawns at last,
making clear what all the preparations
and waiting meant.
The miracle has happened after all:
it is the birth of Christ,
which took place nearly 2,000 years ago,
but still happens in the hearts of men
every Christmas of every year.

"The age of miracles past?"
wrote Thomas Carlyle.
"The age of miracles is forever here!"
Faith in miracles is the true magic of Christmas.

The Life Book of Christmas, Volume Three
The Merriment of Christmas
courtesy Time-Life Books

BECAUSE I KNOW

The best way to put Christ into Christmas
is to put Christ into the heart.
Then I can even enjoy
being pushed around the department stores.
Because I know "He's coming."

John Crosby
"Sounding Board"
U.S. Catholic

HE'S REAL

The doors were locked,
but Jesus came and stood among them and said,
"Peace be with you."

John 20:19

. . . I started reading the New Testament.
    Dylan was right, because I began discovering that
    all the truths I sought
    were contained in the life of this Man
    who was being described in the New Testament.
    It was fantastic . . .
    He set a good example, but it never occurred to me
    that He could really be the Son of God . . .

Then I was backstage during a concert in Austin . . .
walking along *click clack, click clack*
across the hall . . .
and there was a cat standing there
in a Navajo jacket with curly blond hair . . .
And he said, "Could I talk to you?" . . .
I sorta walked close to him and said,
"What is it you'd like to talk to me about?" . . .
And he said,
"I want to talk to you about the Lord!"

WHACK! I felt like the time had come.
Somehow this guy
made all the reading in the Scriptures make sense
because he explained to me
that while Jesus Himself did in fact live this life,
Jesus is real.
We talked and I said,
"Well, I know He's real. I mean He *was* real!"
He said, "No.
He *is* a Spirit and He says in the Scriptures,
'Behold I knock; if any man asks me to enter
I will come and dwell within him.' "
And I said,
"What does that mean? I haven't got room there!"
And he said,
"You ask Him to come in and live in your life."

106

PARADIGM

So, wow, I started to pray with him, and I asked
Jesus to come in and take over my life.
And I started to cry and he started to cry . . .

When you say,
"All right, Lord . . . you point out where you want me to go,
what you want me to do"—
even then you are continually being called back
into this world . . . There is a slipping . . .
But once you've seen the Light . . .
you just keep coming back to it."

Paul Stookey
quoted by Bob Combs and Scott Ross
in "Peter, Me & Mary"
Campus Life magazine

We that loved him so, followed him, honoured him,
Lived in his mild and magnificent eye,
Learned his great language, caught his clear accents,
Made him our pattern to live and to die!

Robert Browning
"The Lost Leader"

ALL THE DIFFERENCE

Remember those puzzle pages . . .
of the Sunday newspaper?
Every once in a while they printed a game
that consisted of a picture,
say, of a family on a picnic . . .
Under this simple cartoon scene
there would be a line that said,
"Can you find the picture of the man
hidden in this picnic-scene?"

At first you would not see it.
You would stare,
and you would turn the page upside down
and stare some more.
But then suddenly, the edge of the clouds
became an ear
and a branch of the tree a smiling mouth,
and . . .
there he was—a man.

Once you saw that face, the simple picnic scene
was never quite the same,
for you had met the man. You had seen him.

Faith is something like that.
For Christians there is a man
hidden in every scene,
and his name is Jesus.

Once he has been met and seen,
no scene, no "seeing,"
is quite the same again.

James Carroll
Prayer From Where You Are

WHADAYA
GOT PLANNED, OLD MAN?

I saw *Cool Hand Luke*
and Paul Newman played a wild character
who courted disaster all his life.
He had no goal, no fear,
and toward the end of his life
he escaped from prison two or three times.

The last time he escaped, he came upon a church
and went in and got on his knees and
said something like,
"Old Man, whadaya got planned for me?
What's next, Old Man?
Whadaya want me to do?
What did you put me on earth for, Old Man?"

I ask the same questions.
I often wonder where my life is heading,
and what's my pupose here on earth . . .
I feel there's got to be more to life . . .
There's got to be some reason to it.

Many people never take control of their own lives,
never say this is the way it's going to be
and maybe I'm one of them.

I didn't come up with any answers this morning.
I just thought about it for a while.

Jerry Kramer
Instant Replay: The Green Bay Diary
of Jerry Kramer

CHECK ONE

Many of us
never take control of our lives.
We don't say to ourselves:
"This is the way it is going to be from now on."
Why?

Maybe we fear to change.
We are afraid that change
will take all the joy out of our lives.
Is this because we really don't trust Jesus
when he says:
"I have come that you may have life
and have it more abundantly." (John 10:10)

Maybe we have tried to change, but failed
and have lost confidence that we can really
change.
Perhaps, we have never taken seriously
Jesus' words:
"With me you can do all things."

Maybe we don't feel any need to change.
There is nothing really wrong with our lives,
we say.
Have we, perhaps, forgotten that Scripture says:
"If we say that we have no sin, we deceive ourselves
and there is no truth in us." (I John 1:8)

Each one of us has his own reasons
for not taking control of his life.

TAKE THE FLOOD

There is a tide
  in the affairs of men,
Which, taken at the flood,
  leads on to fortune;
Omitted,
  all the voyage of their life
Is bound in shallows
  and in miseries.

On such a full sea
  are we now afloat;
And we must take the current
  when it serves,
Or lose our ventures.

William Shakespeare
Julius Caesar, IV, iii

CALLING?

So it may be that
Christ is calling those of us
who have tasted His new wine
to stay at home, right where we are,
and be wholly His people there.

And perhaps
for the first time in our lives
we will find that we have truly . . .
come Home.

Keith Miller
The Taste of New Wine

112

LET THE CHILDREN LAUGH

Let the children have their night of fun and laughter,
let the gifts of Father Christmas delight their play.
Let us grown-ups share to the full
in their unstinted pleasures . . .
resolved that by our sacrifice and daring
these same children shall not be robbed
of their inheritance
or denied their right to live in a free and decent world.

Winston Churchill,
Speech to the American people
during a wartime visit in 1941

WHAT SHALL WE GIVE THE CHILDREN

It seems certain
that they will travel roads
we never thought of,
navigate strange seas,
cross unimagined boundaries,
and glimpse horizons
beyond our power to visualize.
What can we give them
to take along?
For the wild shore of Beyond,
no toy or bauble will do.
It must be something more,
constructed of stouter fabric
discovered among the cluttered
aisles and tinseled bargain
counters of experience,
winnowed from what little
we have learned.
It must be devised out of
responsibility and profound
caring—a homemade present
of selfless love.
Everything changes but the
landscape of the heart.

"What Shall We Give
the Children?"
McCalls magazine

113

PICK A SEED

Jesus' words are like seeds.
Some seeds fall on a path.
These are like people who hear Jesus' words,
but ignore them.
The words do not take root.

Some seeds fall on poor soil.
These are like people who hear Jesus' words
and welcome them.
But the words do not really sink in.
Thus, when the first crunch comes,
the words are abandoned.

Some seeds fall among thorns.
These are like people who welcome Jesus' words.
But the words get snuffed out slowly and subtly
by the day-to-day concerns of life.

Finally, some seeds fall on good soil.
These are like people who hear Jesus' words
and translate them into immediate action.
These people change themselves and the world
they live in.

Mark 4: 15–20 (Paraphrased)

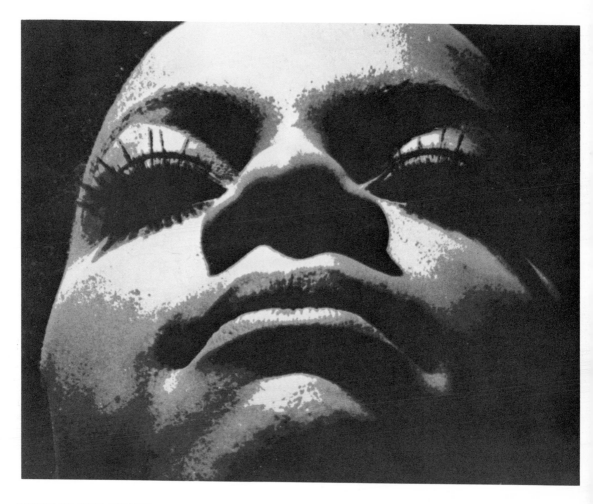

HOPE IN THE HEART

The past decade
has been a most exciting one.
In spite of
the tensions and uncertainties of this period
something profoundly meaningful is taking place.
Old systems of exploitation and oppression
are passing away;
new systems of justice and equality
are being born.
In a real sense this is a great time to be alive.

Therefore,
I am not yet discouraged about the future.
Granted that the easygoing optimism of yesterday
is impossible. Granted that we face
a world crisis which leaves us standing so often
amid the surging murmur of life's restless sea.

But every crisis
has both its dangers and its opportunities.
It can spell either salvation or doom.
In a dark, confused world
the kingdom of God
may yet reign in the hearts of men.

Martin Luther King, Jr.
Strength to Love

THE YOUNGEST

For is he not
the secret of it all—the new,
untried, unblemished
vessel of all possiblity
could he not wax and
grow and come to
man's estate and lead us
down new paths of
goodness? Inherent in the
downey head, sleep-crumpled
face, and starfish hand,
the awakening spirit, lies
man's hope . . .

Margaret Cousins
"A Garland of Wishes
for the Seven Ages of Christmas"
McCalls magazine

LOVE

Let those love now, who never
lov'd before:
Let those who always lov'd,
now love the more.

Anonymous

CHRISTMAS PRAYER

O God, our loving Father,
help us rightly to remember the birth of Jesus,
that we may share in the song of the angels,
the gladness of the shepherds
and the worship of the wise men. . . .

May the Christmas morning make us happy
to be thy children
and the Christmas evening bring us to our beds
with grateful thoughts,
forgiving and forgiven, for Jesus' sake.
Amen.

Robert Louis Stevenson
"Christmas Prayer"

PLEASE LOOK

The gloom of the world
is but a shadow.
Behind it, yet within reach, is joy.
There is radiance
and glory in the darkness,
could we but see,
and to see, we have only to look.
I beseech you
to look.

Fra Giovanni
16th Century